W9-CEU-750

Math All Around Numbers on the Street

Jennifer Rozines Roy and Gregory Roy

 **Marshall Cavendish**
Benchmark
New York

A **number** can tell "how many" or "which one." Numbers are not just used in math. They are found all around us.

Come on! Let's search the city for numbers!

The sign says "WALK." Here we go, across the street. Can you find the numbers on cars, signs, and buildings?

Numbers are made up of **digits**. Digits are the figures **1**, **2**, **3**, **4**, **5**, **6**, **7**, **8**, **9**, and **0**. Using these ten digits, we can make any number in the world.

What digits do you see?

People are standing on line outside the movie theater. Can you count them?

Counting is saying numbers in order. You begin counting objects at **1** and keep going until every one has been counted. The last number is how many objects there are in all.

How many people are wearing hats?

Beep! Beep! Three buses are driving this way. Each bus has ten passengers riding inside.

Another way to show the number of people riding in the three buses is by using **place value**. Place value shows which place each digit is in.

There are **3** sets of **10** passengers. The digit **3** goes in the "tens" place.

3 tens = **30**
|
TENS
PLACE

There are thirty passengers riding the buses today.

One bus stops at the bus stop. Five more people get on the bus. Now there is one set of ten passengers, plus five new riders.

The digit **1** goes in the "tens" place.

$$\underline{\textbf{1}} \; \underline{\;\;}$$

One set of ten passengers

TENS
PLACE

The number of new riders is less than **10**. So that digit goes in the "ones" place.

$$\underline{\textbf{1}} \; \underline{\textbf{5}}$$

Five new riders

ONES
PLACE

Off goes the bus, with fifteen passengers inside!

The bus ride costs $1.25. This boy pays with one dollar and five nickels. Each nickel is 5¢. The boy counts, "**5, 10, 15, 20, 25**."

Counting by skipping over numbers is called **skip-counting**. You can skip-count by twos: **2, 4, 6, 8, 10**, or by threes: **3, 6, 9, 12, 15**, or by any other number.

The boy with the nickels skip-counted by fives.

Soon the boy is at his stop. He gets off the bus on the street where he lives. He walks past the houses until he reaches number **10**. He's home!

The homes on this side of the street are numbered with **even numbers**. Even numbers can be divided by **2**.

Across the street from the boy's house are houses with **odd numbers**. Odd numbers cannot be divided evenly by **2**.

Is the number of your house odd or even?

Look at any street. Numbers are everywhere. The numbers can be single digits.

Or they can have many digits and be greater than nine.

Numbers help us to tell one thing from another and how much money something costs.

Numbers also let us know the size of things

and the time of day or night.

Numbers help us know which way to go and how far to go.

They also show us how fast to go!

Numbers are an important part of our lives, as you can see. How do you use numbers in *your* life?

Glossary

counting—Saying numbers in order.

digit—One of the numbers 1, 2, 3, 4, 5, 6, 7, 8, 9, or 0.

even number—Any number that can be divided by 2; a number found by skip-counting from the number 2.

number—A word that tells "how many"; a symbol that represents an amount.

odd number—Any number that cannot be divided by 2; a number found by skip-counting from the number 1.

place value—The value of the place of a digit in a number.

skip-counting—Counting by "jumping over" or skipping numbers.

Read More

Pluckrose, Henry, *Numbers*. Chicago: Children's Press, 1995.

Scholastic Explains Math Homework. New York: Scholastic, 1998.

Web Sites

Flashcards for Kids
http://edu4kids.com/math

Funbrain
www.funbrain.com

The Math Forum: Ask Dr. Math
http://mathforum.com/dr.math

Index

Page numbers in **boldface** are illustrations.

About the Authors

Jennifer Rozines Roy is the author of more than twenty books. A former Gifted and Talented teacher, she holds degrees in psychology and elementary education.

Gregory Roy is a civil engineer who has co-authored several books with his wife. The Roys live in upstate New York with their son Adam.

Marshall Cavendish Benchmark
99 White Plains Road
Tarrytown, New York 10591-9001
www.marshallcavendish.us

Library of Congress Cataloging-in-Publication Data

Roy, Jennifer Rozines, 1967-
Numbers on the street / by Jennifer Rozines Roy and Gregory Roy.
p. cm. — (Math all around)
Summary: "Reinforces number identification, counting, and reading skills, stimulates critical thinking,
and provides students with an understanding of math in the real world"—Provided by publisher.
Includes bibliographical references and index.
ISBN 0-7614-2002-9
ISBN-13 978-0-7614-2002-6
1. Numeracy—Juvenile literature. 2. Number concept—Juvenile literature.
3. Counting—Juvenile literature. 4. Arithmetic—Juvenile literature.
I. Roy, Gregory. II. Title. III. Series.
QA141.3.R69 2005
513—dc22
2005003523

Photo Research by Anne Burns Images

Cover Photo by *Corbis/*Michael S. Yamashita

The photographs in this book are used with permission and through the courtesy of:
Jay Mallin: pp. 1, 6, 10, 13, 14, 17, 19, 20, 22, 23. *Corbis*: p. 2 Gail Mooney; p. 5 Reuters; p. 9 Royalty Free;
p. 18 O'Brien Productions; p. 21 Najlah Feanny; p. 24 Mike McQueen; p. 25 Alan Schein Photography; p. 26 Jerry Tobias.

Series design by Virginia Pope

Printed in Malaysia
3 5 6 4 2